BOSTON ROB'S FAMILY FAVORITES

COOKBOOK

BOSTON ROB'S FAMILY FAVORITES

COOKBOOK

BY ROBERT C. MARIANO

R. & A. Mariano Inc.

1

Boston Rob's Family Favorites, 1ST EDITION

Copyright © 2020 Robert C. Mariano

Published by R. & A. Mariano Inc.

ISBN: 978-0-9893386-3-9

Author
Robert Mariano

Photography
Hayley Hochstetler

Contributors
Tana Karnchanakphan
Hayley Hochstetler
Mark Slatcher

Edited by
Mark Slatcher

Cover design and book layout by 8131Media

This book is dedicated to my family

Whose love and support

Has allowed me to pursue all of my

Dreams, adventures, and endeavors.

BOSTON ROB'S

FAMILY

FAVORITES

I suppose most of you only think of *Survivor* when you think of me. But you might be surprised to know that I have had a lifelong passion and love for cooking. I grew up in a traditional Italian-American family that believed in having family dinners together. My parents both cooked and all of us participated in preparing and enjoying family meals. As far as I can remember, none of us ever complained about this. We enjoyed cooking together. Most of the time it involved a lot of kidding around; but there were plenty of meaningful, insightful conversations, too.

I think there's something to be said for passing down the art of the family dinner that is being lost in the world we live in now. It is so fast-paced, we've evolved into an eat-on-the-run society. There is a joyful beauty in cooking with the people you care about. It can be as simple as the family getting together to watch the big game and sharing some sandwiches. Or waking up on a Saturday with Amber and the kids and having pancakes—and staying in our pajamas 'til noon. Of course, if you also prepare delicious foods you'll be fulfilled mind, body, and soul.

Let me tell you a story; after my appearance on *Survivor: Marquesas* I did the talk show circuit. One of them gifted me a trip to Sicily and I was allowed to bring a guest; I took my dad. The first night I was jet lagged because of the time difference and I woke up late in the evening. I was starving but my dad was asleep so I ventured out into the streets of Palermo alone.

Not too far away I discovered a small pizza shop. I placed my order and he cooked it fresh—to my amazement—in less than three minutes. They had a tiny brick oven he said was 1400°F. It was the best pizza I ever had in my life. I took it back to the hotel and when my dad woke up we shared it. It's a fond memory that ignited a spark within me.

When I got home, I went to work on my own pizza recipe. I began with one passed down to me from my Nonina, my father's mother. She was born in Italy and she came to the United States before my father was born. She was the matriarch of the family and an exceptional cook. The memories I have of the meals she made I'll never forget. She was one of a kind! To achieve the flavor and texture of the pizza I remember from Sicily, I experimented with all kinds of ovens and temperatures, as well as ingredients and toppings. By the end, I managed to create a pizza that takes me back to the streets of Palermo and keeps me in my grandmother's kitchen at the same time. I have to say, the sun-ripened San Marzano tomatoes and the extra virgin olive oil really make this pizza recipe sing.

I've never sought any professional training but I have experimented substantially to perfect my recipes. What you'll find on the following pages are our favorite dishes. I hope you enjoy them with your families as we have.

- Robert "Boston Rob" Mariano

BREAK-
FAST

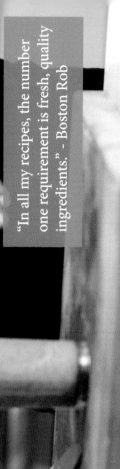

THE GOOD MORNING SMOOTHIE

INGREDIENTS

2 Small Organic Bananas
3 oz Fresh Spinach
1 tbsp Hemp Seed
1 tbsp Flax Seed
1 tbsp Chia Seed
4 oz Fresh Organic Blueberries
12 oz Unsweetened Almond Milk
12 oz Cubed Ice
3 sprigs Mint
1 Orange (for garnish)

(S E R V E S   T W O)

HOW TO

STEP ONE

Place the ice into the blender.
Add the spinach followed by the blueberries and bananas cut in half.

STEP TWO

Snap the sprigs of mint three times and add to the blender.
Drop in the Hemp, Flax, and Chia seeds.
Pour in the almond milk.

STEP THREE

Blend together until smooth.
Pour and garnish with an orange slice.

INGREDIENTS

2 Large Brown Eggs
2 cups All-Purpose Flour
1¾ cups Milk
½ cup Vegetable Oil
1 tbsp Sugar
4 tsp Baking Powder
¼ tsp Salt
½ tsp Vanilla Extract
12 slices Applewood Bacon

(MAKES SIX)

HOW TO

STEP ONE

Preheat the oven to 375°F. Place a cooling rack in a baking sheet. Lay out the bacon on the rack and bake for 25 minutes or until desired crispiness.

STEP TWO

Preheat the waffle iron. Crack eggs into a large mixing bowl and whisk until fluffy. Add flour, milk, vegetable oil, sugar, baking powder, salt, and vanilla. Whisk until smooth.

STEP THREE

Coat the waffle iron with a non-stick cooking spray. Pour in batter, criss-cross the bacon on top. Cook until golden brown.

CARINA'S BACON
WAFFLES

ISABETTA'S
HOMEMADE
MUSELI

(SERVES TWO)

INGREDIENTS

½ cup Raw Rolled Oats
1 Large Honeycrisp Apple, halved
1 tbsp Raw Cashews
1 tbsp Dried Cranberries
1 tbsp Roasted and Salted Shelled
    Pumpkin Seeds
1 tbsp Sunflower Seeds
1 tbsp Walnuts
1 tbsp Mini Semi-Sweet Milk
    Chocolate Chips
⅓ cup Frozen Blueberries
8 oz Almond Milk

HOW TO

STEP ONE

In a large mixing bowl, add all of the dry ingredients.
Cut the apple in half, dice, and set aside.

STEP TWO

Gently mix the dry ingredients together and separate
into two bowls.
Add half of the frozen blueberries and half of the diced
apple pieces to each bowl.
Pour almond milk into each bowl and serve.

"Isabetta is the most adventur-
ous eater of all my children.
She'll try anything and she
loves anchovies, just like her
father." - Boston Rob

AMBER'S BLUEBERRY PANCAKES

1 cup All-Purpose Flour
1 tbsp Sugar
2 tsp Baking Powder
½ tsp Salt
1 Large Egg
¾ cup Milk
¼ cup Butter, melted
4 oz fresh Organic Blueberries

(MAKES EIGHT)

H O W   T O

S T E P   O N E

In a mixing bowl, add flour, sugar, baking powder, and salt.
Add melted butter, milk, and egg.

S T E P   T W O

Mix into a batter. On a greased pan, pour about 1/4 cup of the batter.
Sprinkle with blueberries on top.
Flip the pancake when bubbles start to form.

S T E P   T H R E E

Cook until both sides are golden brown. Serve hot.

"My kids are the luckiest kids in the world to have Amber as their mother, and so am I as my wife. She supports me in all my endeavors and makes it possible for me to go on all my crazy adventures." - Boston Rob

SAND-
WICHES

HOW TO

Preheat the panini press or pan. Butter two slices of bread; place one slice on the press/pan, buttered-side down. Layer the following ingredients in order: provolone, bacon, mozzarella, cheddar, tomato, Gruyère, bacon, and basil.

Top with the second slice of bread, buttered-side up. Drizzle with olive oil; add a pinch of salt and pepper. Place into the panini press for four minutes; or turn in a pan until both sides are golden brown. Let rest for one minute before serving.

THE MURLONIO GRILLED CHEESE

"Amber and I found love in a unique place where most people would never expect it, in a game where you're supposed to vote each other out. In all of that chaos we found each other and fell in love. " - Boston Rob

MEATBALL SUB

"My culinary choices are influenced by all the wonderful places I've been able to visit in my life. Rooted in my traditional Italian upbringing and enhanced by all the traveling I've been fortunate enough to enjoy." - Boston Rob

INGREDIENTS

2 lbs Ground Beef

1 lb Ground Pork

3 Large Eggs

2 sprigs chopped Italilan Parseley

2 tbsp Extra Virgin Olive Oil

1 tsp Sea Salt

1 tsp Pepper

1 cup Bread Crumbs

½ cup Pecorino Romano Cheese

Homemade Red Sauce

6 Sub-Rolls

(MAKES EIGHTEEN)

24

HOW TO

STEP ONE

Preheat the oven to 375°F. In a large mixing bowl, combine the ground beef with ground pork. Add eggs, ⅓ cup Pecorino Romano cheese, chopped parsely, olive oil, breadcrumbs, salt and pepper.

STEP TWO

Lightly spray two baking sheets with non-stick oil. Mix the ingredients by hand and roll into two-inch diameter balls. Place onto baking sheets one inch apart. Bake for 30 minutes or until the internal temperature reaches 165°F.

STEP THREE

Slice the roll and place three meatballs inside. Top with sauce and grated Pecorino Romano cheese.

"There is a joyful beauty in cooking with the people you care about. It can be as simple as the family getting together to watch the big game and sharing some sandwiches." - Boston Rob

HOW TO

STEP ONE

Preheat the oven to 350°F. Cut sausage links into thirds. Deseed peppers and chop. Peel and slice the onions. Place sausages, peppers, and onions into a mixing bowl. Add olive oil. Salt and pepper to taste. Gently toss all of the ingredients.

STEP TWO

Place ingredients into a two-quart casserole dish. Cover and bake for 45 minutes. Remove cover, bake for an additional 15 minutes or until the links reach an internal temperature of 165°F. Slice the baguette, spoon in the sausage mixture, and top with provolone cheese.

GAMEDAY ITALIAN SAUSAGE SANDWICH

INGREDIENTS

1 Green, Yellow, Red Pepper
1 Large Sweet Onion
1½ lbs Italian Sausage
1 French Baguette
2 tsp Extra Virgin Olive Oil
Sliced Sharp Provolone
Salt and Pepper

(SERVES FOUR)

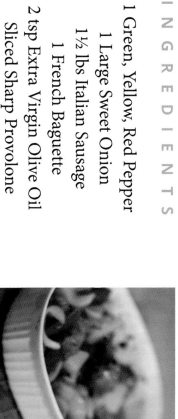

SALADS AND STARTERS

H O W   T O

Wash and quarter the tomatoes. Plate the Burrata and tomatoes. Drizzle with olive oil. Salt and pepper to taste. Top with fresh basil.

Layer prosciutto. Drizzle with balsamic glaze. Serve chilled.

I N G R E D I E N T S

4 medium Heirloom Beefsteak Tomatoes

2 - 4 oz balls Burrata

1 oz Basil

2 oz Prosciutto

Extra Virgin Olive Oil

Balsamic Glaze

Salt and Pepper

(S E R V E S   F O U R)

"I think there's something to be said for passing down the art of the family dinner that is being lost in the world we live in now." - Boston Rob

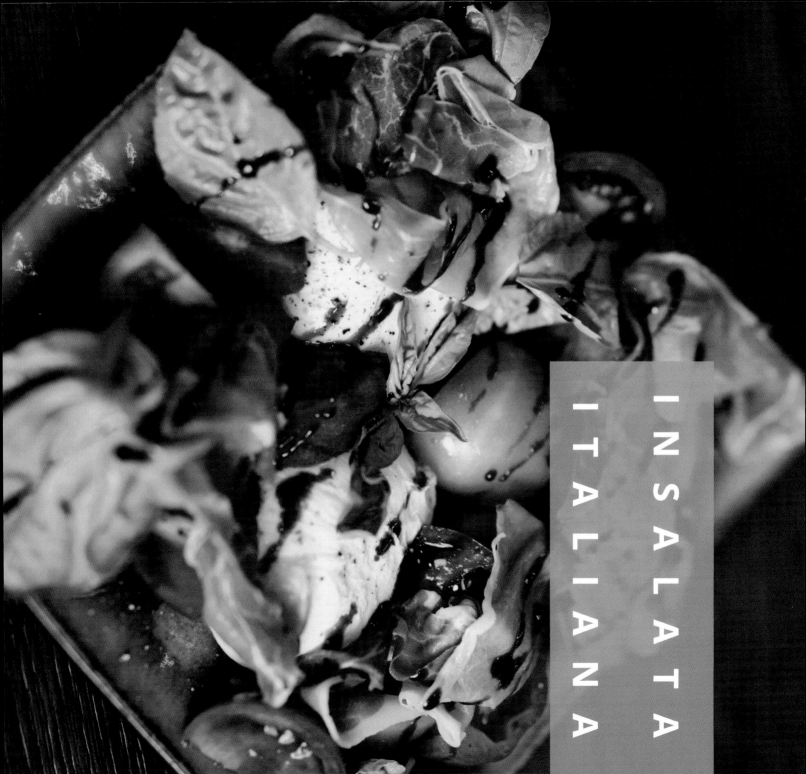

INSALATA ITALIANA

SUMMER BEACH SALAD

1 small Seedless Watermelon

1 oz Spinach

½ cup Pecans

3½ oz Italian Gorgonzola

6 oz Mandarin Oranges (drained)

1 pint small Heirloom tomatoes

Olive Oil

Salt and Pepper

(S E R V E S   F O U R)

"If you're going to eat pizza, pasta, ribeye, and Zeppole—like we do—once in a while you'd better throw in a salad or a smoothie. " - Boston Rob

H O W   T O

Rinse spinach and place in an oversized mixing bowl. Drizzle with olive oil. Dice watermelon into ½ inch cubes. Place watermelon, pecans, and tomatoes into a bowl. Crumble the gorgonzola on top and toss. Salt and pepper to taste.

Plate the salad on a chilled dish. Top with Mandarin oranges. Serve chilled.

THE MARIANO CHARCUTERIE BOARD

At every family get together we had when I was a kid, there would always be a cold-cut platter and it was usually provided by my Uncle Jimmy's bakery. Since the sixties, he has operated the B.C. Baking Company in Hyde Park, MA. Every time I go back to visit, I never miss a chance to go by the bakery. In addition to making fresh breads there, they make sandwiches, pizzas, pastries, cannoli...the list goes on and they still also make cold-cut platters. This charcuterie board is a nod to Uncle Jimmy's old school platters.

"As a kid we always had a garden at our house. At a minimum, we grew tomatoes and basil. The difference in flavor between a garden-fresh tomato and one you pick up at a supermarket can only be known if you've grown them yourself." - Boston Rob

MEATS

Capocollo
Genoa Salami
Prosciutto
Soppressata

CHEESES

Raw Milk Cheddar
Gorgonzola
Chipotle Gouda
Gruyère

EXTRAS

Almonds
Cashews
Dried Cranberries
Honeycomb
Olives w/ Bleu Cheese

EXTRAS

Fresh Raspberries
Fresh Blueberries
Fresh Blackberries
Roasted Red Bell Peppers
Artichoke Hearts

35

MAIN COURSES

SPAGHETTI ALGIO OLIO

1 lb Spaghetti

6 cloves Garlic

1 tsp Crushed Red Pepper

¼ cup fresh chopped Flat Leaf Parsley

2 tbsp Butter

¼ cup Extra Virgin Olive Oil

Parmigiano Reggiano

Salt and Pepper

(S E R V E S   F O U R)

H O W   T O

S T E P   O N E

Boil six quarts of water in a pot and salt generously. Cook the pasta *al dente* and <u>do not</u> strain or dispose of the water. As the pasta cooks, heat up a pan on low. Peel and smash six cloves of garlic and thinly slice. Add olive oil, butter, crushed red pepper, and garlic to the pan. Cook on low for ten minutes.

S T E P   T W O

Use tongs to transfer the pasta from the pot to the pan. Add one cup of pasta water to the pan. Add parsley and stir. Plate the pasta and grate Parmigiano Reggiano as desired.

"Put the garlic in while the oil is cold so you toast the garlic without burning it"
- Boston Rob

"If you told me I had to pick just one food I could eat for the rest of my life, it would be pizza." - Boston Rob

INGREDIENTS

PIZZA

1 lb pizza dough
4 oz Capocollo
8 oz fresh Mozzarella
8 leaves Basil

SAUCE

28 oz can whole peeled
San Marazano Tomatoes
1 tsp Salt
1 tsp Pepper
1 tbsp Oregano
3 tbsp Extra Virgin Olive Oil
2 tsp Garlic Powder
1 tsp Onion Powder

ADELINA'S OVEN-BAKED PIZZA

HOW TO

SAUCE

Pour tomatoes in a large mixing bowl. Crush the tomatoes by hand. Mix in the spices and olive oil.

PIZZA

Preheat oven to 450°F. Stretch the dough the length of a baking sheet. Drizzle with extra virgin olive oil on both sides. Ladle the sauce onto the dough; spread close to the edge. Break up the Mozzarella and spread evenly on the dough. Do the same with the capocollo and basil leaves. Drizzle olive oil over the pizza and place into the oven. Bake for 15 minutes; rotate halfway through.

41

HOW TO

INGREDIENTS

8 oz Salmon Filet
2 tbsp Extra Virgin Olive Oil
4 oz Spinach
4 cloves Garlic
½ pint Grape Tomatoes, sliced
1 tsp Crushed Red Pepper
Salt and Pepper

STEP ONE

Coat both sides of the filet with olive oil, salt and pepper generously. Peel and dice the cloves of garlic. Heat a pan on medium and add olive oil. Toast the garlic for two minutes. Add tomatoes, spinach, and crushed red pepper. Salt and pepper to taste. Sauté the spinach until wilted.

STEP TWO

Fire the grill to medium-high heat. Grill salmon for eight minutes.

(Optional) Serve with a side of rice.

"Lucia doesn't get excited by a big juicy ribeye; but ever since she was little she's loved fish, especially salmon." - Boston Rob

42

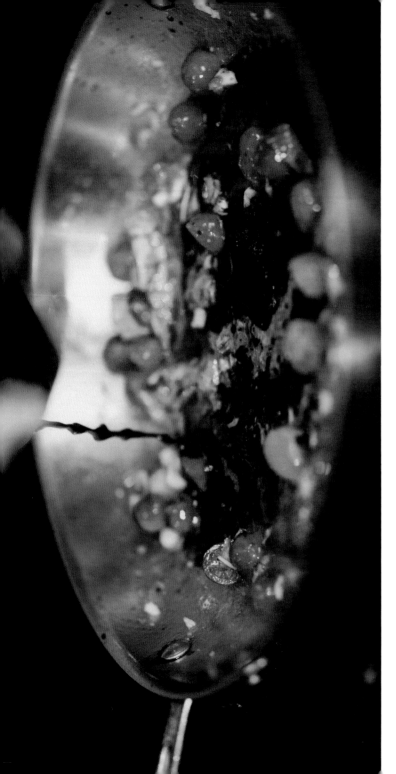

HOW TO

Rinse, trim, and butterfly the filets. Season the chicken on both sides with salt and pepper. Peel and smash six cloves of garlic; chop thin. Remove the stems and coarsely chop the basil. Heat a frying pan to medium and add two tablespoons of olive oil.

Sauté the filets to an internal temperature of 165°F (roughly six minues per side). Remove the filets and set on a paper towel. Add the garlic, tomatoes, and half of the basil to the hot pan. Sauté for three minutes. Add a tablespoon each of olive oil and balsamic vinegar. Simmer for three minutes. Return the chicken to the pan and coat each side with the glaze. Add remaining basil and reduce heat to low. Place mozzarella on each piece of chicken. Cover for five minutes and then plate.

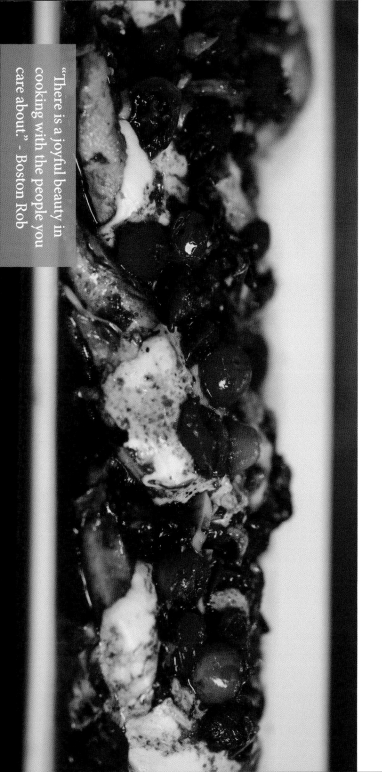

> "There is a joyful beauty in cooking with the people you care about." - Boston Rob

SUNDAY NIGHT CHICKEN CAPRESE

(SERVES FOUR)

INGREDIENTS

1½ lbs organic skinless Chicken Filets

6 cloves Garlic

½ pint Grape Tomatoes, sliced

1 oz Basil

6 oz Mozzarella

3 tbsp Extra Virgin Olive Oil

3 tbsp Balsamic Vinegar

Salt and Pepper

INGREDIENTS

1 - 8 oz Ribeye Steak
1 Garlic Bulb, cut in half
2 tbsp Butter
2 sprigs Rosemary
4 sprigs Thyme
Salt and Pepper

HOW TO

STEP ONE

Set the steak out one hour prior to cooking. Salt and pepper each side generously. Heat grill to high.

STEP TWO

Place the steak onto the grill. Cook for four minutes on each side. At the same time, place a cast iron pan on the grill.

STEP THREE

Add butter, rosemary, thyme, and garlic halves to the pan. Move the steak to the pan and spoon melted butter over each side. Cook an additional three minutes per side. Let rest for ten minutes before serving.

BOSTON
ROB'S
RIBEYE

SWEET TREATS

"The Zeppole is akin to a Beignet with confectionary sugar on top. When I was a kid, and now with my own kids, it was something we would traditionally make on Christmas Eve." – Boston Rob

ITALIAN ZEPPOLE

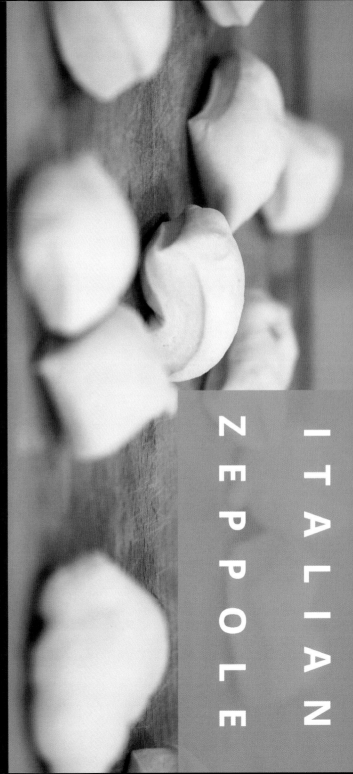

INGREDIENTS

1 lb Bread Dough

2 cups Vegetable Oil

Confectionary Sugar

4 oz Provolone Cheese (optional)

1 jar Anchovies (optional)

(MAKES SIXTEEN)

HOW TO

STEP ONE

Set out dough an hour prior to bring to room temperature. Cut dough into sixteen pieces.

Optional: Wrap each dough piece around a slice of provolone or anchovy.

STEP TWO

In a circular frying pan, add vegetable oil and bring to 350°F. Place dough pieces into the pan. Turn each piece until both sides are golden brown. Remove from pan and place onto a plate lined with a paper towel. Dust with confectionary sugar (unless filled with provolone or anchovy).

MA'S MAGIC BARS

HOW TO

Preheat the oven to 350°F. Grease an 11" x 9" glass baking pan. Crush the graham crackers until fine. Mix with melted butter, cinnamon, and sugar. Press the graham cracker mixture into the bottom of the pan.

Layer chocolate chips and walnuts. Top with shredded coconut. Pour the entire can of sweetened condensed milk on top. Bake for 25 minutes or until golden brown.

"This recipe was passed down from my grandmother Helen to my mother Linda, and from my mother to my children. It's my family's go-to dessert for any occasion." - Boston Rob

INGREDIENTS

2 cups Graham Crackers
1 stick melted Butter
¼ cup Sugar
¾ semisweet mini Chocolate Chips
1 cup chopped Walnuts
¼ cup Shredded Coconut
1 cup Sweetened Condensed Milk
1 tbsp Cinnamon

ISLAND
FAVOR-
ITES

"One of the catchphrases of the show is, 'Fire is life,' and it truly is. You have warmth and the ability to cook food."
– Boston Rob

FIREMAKING

101

Coconut Husk
Twigs
Wood logs

TOOLS

Machete
Flint

HOW TO

Gather coconut husk for tinder and assemble the twigs for a fire. Scrape some magnesium from the back of the flint onto the tinder pile. Strike the flint onto the tinder. When a small fire starts to take, move the lit tinder to the twigs. Give the flame plenty of air.

HOW TO

Remove coconut husk and shell. Split and dice the coconut. Place coconut in a cast iron pan. Place the pan on top of the open fire. Add water to the pan. Squeeze a lime over the coconut and add salt to taste. Cook until charred and tender.

"I readily admit that this dish isn't for everyone. A few have even called it inedible. But when Amber and I make it at home, to us it tastes just like it did on the island. And to us, it's delicious." – Boston Rob

FIRE-ROASTED COCONUT LIME POPCORN

CASTAWAY

CRISPY RICE

H O W T O

Place a cast iron pan on the fire. Add 1 cup of water and bring to boil. Add ½ cup of rice and cover the pan. Move the pan to a lower heat section of the fire for 20 minutes. Remove the cover and put the pan back on the fire. Stir and cook until crispy and slightly charred. Add lime and salt to taste.

"On the island, it wasn't unusual for us to toast all of the rice. Having something warm to eat, something that tasted different with its char-grilled flavor, made a tremendous difference when you're getting rained on day after day." - Boston Rob

GRAZIE!